Teach Kids to Become Mentally Strong

How to Instill a Strong Mentality in Your Kids and Help Them Overcome Struggles and Achieve Success in a Stigmatized World

Frank Dixon

Before we begin, I have something special waiting for you. An action-packed 1 page printout with a few quick & easy tips taken from this book that you can start using today to become a better parent right now!

It's my gift to you, free of cost. Think of it as my way of saying thank you to you for purchasing this book.

Claim your download of Profoundly Positive Parenting with Frank Dixon by scanning the QR code below and join my mailing list.

Sign up below to grab your free copy, print it out and hang it on the fridge!

Sign Up By Scanning The QR Code With Your Phone's Camera To Be Redirected To A Page To Enter Your Email And Receive INSTANT Access To Your Download

Before we jump in, I'd like to express my gratitude. I know this mustn't be the first book you came across and yet you still decided to give it a read. There are numerous courses and guides you could have picked instead that promise to make you an ideal and well-rounded parent while raising your children to be the best they can be.

But for some reason, mine stood out from the rest and this makes me the happiest person on the planet right now. If you stick with it, I promise this will be a worthwhile read.

In the pages that follow, you're going to learn the best parenting skills so that your child can grow to become the best version of themselves and in doing so experience a meaningful understanding of what it means to be an effective parent.

Notable Quotes About Parenting

*"Children Must Be Taught How To Think,
Not What To Think."*

— **Margaret Mead**

**"It's easier to build strong children than to fix
broken men [or women]."**

- Frederick Douglass

**"Truly great friends are hard to find, difficult
to leave, and impossible to forget."**

— George Randolf

**"Nothing in life is to be feared, it is only to be
understood. Now is the time to understand
more, so that we may fear less."**

— Scientist Marie Curie

Table of Contents

Introduction

"Oh, you're just being a bit dramatic. You just need to get out more and have some fun."

Sometimes, we are not fine. We don't need friends to walk all over us telling us that we are being sensitive or emotional. Mental health issues are real and so is the stigma around them. Stigma is defined as a negative and unfair social attitude toward an individual or group. It often puts shame on someone for a perceived deficiency or difference. Mental health stigmas include societal disapproval. It is when society decides to put down someone based on an illness or condition that they have been accompanied by emotional distress such as anxiety and stress.

Stigmatization of mental illnesses usually comes from family, friends, partners, and co-workers. Stigmatization makes the sufferer experience guilt for being different, prevents them from getting help, and struggles leading comfortable lives. Stigmas around mental health come from simplified or generalized beliefs that are often negative, inaccurate, or offensive. Stigmas cause people to make quick judgments about one another based on some defining characteristics. This often results in the individual with a mental health disorder feeling uneasy, uncomfortable, and invalidated. It's easy to overlook the signs and symptoms of early depression and anxiety or worse—sugarcoat them as "temporary feelings." We are all guilty of doing it at some point in our lives.

We have disregarded a mother's pleas and shamed her when she is suffering from postpartum depression, but this should be the happiest time of your life. You just became a mom for the first time. Why don't you seem joyous? We have told her. We have reminded her that it's selfish of her to feel angry at herself and her newborn. We have told her that crying is just a part of the healing process. We have told her that she would eventually make it past the first five to six weeks after childbirth and then all will be good again. But rarely have we stopped to ask if all she needs is some comfort, sleep, and emotional escape. Instead, we tucked the baby neatly in her lap and expected her to be the best mother there is. This is just an example of the negativity that surrounds mental health issues and our answer to them.

We are quick to tell an office colleague that is still grieving the loss of his wife to just start dating again. We don't listen to our children when they complain of having anxiety and label it as a lack of confidence. We are the first ones to name and shame anybody that doesn't feel joyous like us. We blame them for bringing down everyone's mood with their pessimistic outlook on life. We shame them for not being thankful for the lovely family and friends they have.

The stigma that revolves around mental health issues is what makes it so much harder for troubled souls to seek help. Did you know that 40% of people with mental health issues don't seek professional help because they fear being stigmatized ("Addressing Stigma," n.d.)? In their mind, they blame themselves for being the black sheep. They fear that seeking professional help will make them a laughing stock. They fear that speaking about them would make them come out as an attention-seeking person. They even fear that talking about their troubles will drive their loved ones away.

We judge but don't help. We shame but never offer comfort. We say we will be there for them but aren't when they need us. For someone battling a mental health issue, this confirms their fears about themselves, and they find it easier to just quit. This has to stop before our carelessness and prejudice takes more lives. We have to stop and educate ourselves so that we can be better partners, parents, and support systems for our families. We have to be more open with our children and encourage expression so that they don't end up suffering from a mental health condition.

Chapter 1:

Raising Mentally-Strong

Kids in a Stigmatized World

Children can develop mental health issues for many reasons. Some are biological or genetic. There is little that can be done about that. However, most mental issues arise when children start school and expand their social circle. As they make new friends, they learn about emotions such as affection, anger, irritation, frustration, and sadness. They feel disheartened when their friend doesn't show up to school. They feel angry when someone says something mean to them. They become anxious when the teacher asks them to present something in front of the whole class.

Some children develop a mental illness due to childhood trauma. Perhaps they witnessed a close one leave or die. Maybe they suffered abuse from their parents, were always compared with another sibling, or were given no attention while growing up. All these bad experiences can take home in the mind and the heart, making children anxious whenever they experience a remotely similar situation.

Some children have trouble navigating their career paths which can lead to stress and anxiety. They have a hard time picking a major because they are unsure about their options. Their anxiety multiplies when everyone around them seems to have a solid idea of what they want to try and do with their lives.

Mental health issues can also stem from violence or environmental injustice. Sometimes, there is no reason why one feels depressed or pessimistic. Regardless of what causes mental health issues among children, they are equally damaging and detrimental to one's health as is cancer, diabetes, or multiple sclerosis. Thus, society cannot and should not take them lightly or worse by treating them as nonsensical. The reason they do is because of the stigmatization that accompanies it, but how can we stop it—if we can?

By raising children to become mentally strong, resilient, and self-confident adults.

Many mental health issues arise when parents neglect their child's emotional needs. Parents ignore or discredit their child's feelings and emotions. For example, telling boys not to cry because "men don't cry" is discrediting their need to vent out their emotions and deal with them as everyone should. By saying this, we are telling them to grow out of it and get their act together. But how can they when all they need is some support and consoling?

Similarly, when young girls want to pursue careers in science and technology, we hush them down by saying these aren't appropriate fields for women and that they should stick with "easy subjects."

Many children with self-esteem issues don't receive the kind of love and affection they deserve. The lack of emotional support increases their doubts about themselves. Such kids start to feel unworthy of love and affection and end up in toxic relationships without any self-respect for themselves. They also develop mental health issues where they are constantly anxious and worried that their partner would leave them for someone more attractive.

Influence is a powerful tool. It's what shapes a resilient mind. Children brought up in households where they are empowered, their opinions valued, and failures seen as lessons are at a better chance to develop a positive and tough mindset. As parents, we must promote assertiveness and raise freethinkers. Our children should know how to solve problems, face setbacks, and bounce back stronger, ultimately having confidence in their skills and abilities. They should have a mind of their own and make responsible choices. They shouldn't worry about what others think of them.

Mentally strong and resilient children are go-getters. They are self-starters and more prepared to deal with whatever life could possibly throw at them. Their character is shaped by the values their parents' practice and the beliefs they have. Therefore, what we say, do, and practice shapes their personality. How we conquer difficult times, the type of relationships we have, and how we face setbacks can say a lot about the type of personality they have.

When we raise confident and resilient children, we enable them to take control of their lives and not settle for anything less than the best. We teach them to set healthy boundaries and confidently say no to things they aren't comfortable doing. We empower them to make sensible decisions and choices concerning them. We allow them to become independent, self-sufficient, and inspired. When we raise mentally strong children, we focus on building their social and life skills.

A mentally strong child knows their place in the world. They don't rely on others to make them feel good about themselves. They are equipped to handle their emotions and not let themselves feel overwhelmed.

Developing such an attitude from the get-go requires a lot of work. For starters, parents need to educate themselves about the many mental health concerns common among tweens and teenagers today. Before anything else, they need to notice the signs of a mental health issue. Let's understand further about it in the next chapters and see how parents can raise mentally strong children in this highly stigmatized world.

Chapter 2:

Educate Yourself and

Others

Although stigmatization around mental health is decreasing in recent years, parents and educators still need to be more educated about the reasons that contribute to it. Only when they can comprehend the extent of it and understand what goes through in the mind of someone with a mental disorder can they take the necessary steps to prevent its progression. One of the best ways to reduce stigmatization of mental health issues is to get in contact with someone diagnosed with one and humanize how they feel. The stigma can also be reduced when we have important conversations about it at home. When we explain to our children how stress and anxiety is only a temporary phase of their lives, they can be more expressive about their issues. Communication can improve when children feel like their issues and concerns aren't brushed under the rug but are instead valid and genuine. Only when we start addressing them and look toward the best treatment options can we help our children heal from them and get better.

It all starts with having an open mind—an issue that seems trivial to you might not look the same to a teenager. Their issues may arise from a lack of confidence in their physical appearance or self-esteem. They may need help with uplifting themselves. Since we are the most influential people in their lives, we have to ensure that they get that source of motivation and encouragement from us. They don't need to hear responses like, "Toughen up" or "Life isn't fair." They need to hear you say things that validate their feelings and concerns. If they feel nervous about an event at school, let them know that you understand how it feels.

Despite being their guardian, mentor, and friend, parents often don't grasp the concept of a mental disorder until it's too late. They recall their childhood and try to compare their child's life with their own experiences growing up. Yet not all experiences are the same. As a parent, you may have had the guts to toughen up, but your child might not.

Failing to recognize or immediately refusing to address a child's mental health struggles can make it harder for them to trust you in the future. Without a strong support system, children may feel lonely. They may find themselves in greater distress. It can make them feel like an outsider in their own family. Let's be honest: Downplaying mental illnesses is fairly common, especially among older members of the family. They don't believe in disorders like depression or anxiety. They will tell you that you need to get out more, make some new friends, and do things that make you happy, but this isn't always the best cure for someone that suffers from deep self-esteem issues about themselves.

Know the Signs of a Mental Illness

Since the ultimate goal is educating yourself and others, the first step for that is to read up on the signs that are associated with a mental disorder. Not every child with a mental health issue exhibits all of these—this is only for starters to let you grasp the idea as to what type of behavior to look for.

Changes in How They Think

Some of the most common signs of a mental health disorder are a change in the way a child perceives themselves and their abilities.

- Are they being too critical about themselves and always have something negative to say about themselves?

- Do they have trouble focusing?

- Are they falling back in class?

- Do they have poor grades?

- Do they blame themselves for things they can't control?

If yes, then there's a chance that they are dealing with some mental health issues.

Changes in How They Feel

Apart from the emotional turmoil that they are in, there are also some changes in their behavior. For instance, things they used to enjoy doing previously might not be of any interest to them anymore. Similarly, they may react to situations differently, too. Look for these signs listed below to confirm your doubts that they don't feel fine.

- Do they exaggerate their reaction and make incidents seem bigger than they are?

- Do they seem unhappy all the time?

- Are their responses filled with sarcasm, irritation, or guilt?

- Do they seem worried, anxious, or fearful?

- Are they hopeless and lonely?

If yes, then there is something on their minds that is bothering them. Do check in with them and have a conversation about how you can make them feel better.

Changes in Their Activities

If your child had a happy-go-lucky nature before and doesn't have one now, it's important to understand what drove away their happiness and confidence in themselves. This is only possible if you can identify the changes in how they spend most of their time doing. For example, do they not want to have friends over or deliberately make excuses to skip going to parties? Do they seem upset over every little thing and start crying about how miserable their life is? Here are some more signs to look for:

- Do they withdraw from sports, activities, and games they normally enjoyed?

- Do they experience sudden outbursts of anger over small issues?

- Are they no longer energetic and enthusiastic about life and possible opportunities?

- Are they quiet most of the time?

- Do they have trouble sleeping or relaxing?

- Are they falling back to less mature behaviors like temper tantrums?

- Do they have trouble getting along with people?

- Are they spending a lot of time daydreaming or being secretive about their life?

Changes in Their Physical State

Sometimes, when anxiety and stress become the norm, it starts to affect not just our mental and emotional state but also our physical. We know this because we have all experienced grief firsthand. We know how it can take a toll on your physical well-being. We understand how stress can make us quit eating or cause binge eating. We know how it can result in constant headaches and fatigue. If you notice any such signs in your child, know that too much stress has taken over their life and they are finding it hard to cope with it. For example, check on the following:

- Do they complain of headaches; neck and shoulder pain; or stomachaches often?

- Do they seem lethargic and tired all the time?

- Are they having problems sleeping well?

- Do you often catch them biting their nails or twisting their hair often?

- Are they losing or gaining weight fast?

- Are they engaging in self-harming behaviors like drinking or smoking?

If yes, then it must be noted that there is something big affecting their lives. It could be a breakup, worry about prospects, or lack of self-esteem. The sooner you identify these signs, the better off you will be at helping them find the right solutions.

Most Common Mental Illnesses Among Tweens and Teens

Once you identify the signs, you need to address the mental health issue so that together, you can work on improving their overall well-being. There are several mental health conditions linked with preteens and teenagers. From being bullied to thinking they aren't good enough to deserving all the good things in life, below are some of the most common mental health disorders among children of today and how they manifest ("Adolescent mental health," 2020):

- **Attention-Deficit/Hyperactivity Disorder (ADHD):** Children with ADHD have trouble with attention. They are hyperactive individuals that have a hard time sitting down and relaxing. They are known to react to things impulsively, leaving little for the mind to comprehend an appropriate response. The most common reasons children develop ADHD are genetic or environmental. They may have it in their genes and be born with it or develop it after going through someone traumatic in their early childhood.

- **Anxiety:** Anxiety affects children coming of age the most. Persistent fears about many things from getting into a good college to going away from home and friends are all reasons causing one to overthink and stress out. According to a survey by the National Institutes of Health, one in three teenagers aged 13 to 18 suffers from an anxiety disorder (McCarthy, 2019). Anxiety can be temporary and related to an issue or chronic. Chronic anxiety can lead to depression and other more severe mental health disorders. There can be different types of anxiety one can experience such as:

  1. **Generalized Anxiety:** With generalized anxiety, a child worries about everyday life events for no reason. For instance, feeling anxious when getting dressed for school, getting on the bus, or going into the class, etc.

  2. **Social Anxiety:** In social anxiety, a child feels like they are always being watched or judged by the people surrounding them. This triggers the

need to be alone or socially distanced from the world.

3. **Obsessive-Compulsive:** In this type of anxiety disorder, children have repeated unwanted sensations and thoughts that drive them to something repetitively.

- **Depression:** Depression is a persistent feeling where one feels sad all the time. Children with depression tend to lose interest in things that hamper their ability to perform at their best. It also affects their relationships with their friends and educators. Some days, they can experience excessive mood swings that can lead to unsafe, self-damaging, and unguarded thoughts.

- **Eating Disorders:** Eating disorders are most common among teenagers. Since teenage years are a time of rapid hormonal changes that cause the body to change, teenagers become conscious of their weight and develop eating disorders like anorexia nervosa, binge eating, or bulimia nervosa. All of these are characterized by harmful eating practices such as eating too much or restricting calories.

- **Episodic Drinking and Substance Abuse:** Drinking and substance abuse are common among teenage males. According to research,

13.6% of males aged 15 to 19 are at risk of developing a drinking problem. Other than that, the use of cannabis and tobacco among teenagers is also a concerning fact for parents. It is estimated that cannabis is the most widely used drug among teenagers today with about 4.7% of 15-year-old teenagers using it at least once ("Adolescent mental health," 2020).

- **Post-Traumatic Stress Disorder (PTSD):** Children suffering from PTSD experience emotional distress, troubling memories, have nightmares, and have disruptive behaviors because of some trauma they suffered in the past. Mostly, the trauma is linked with abuse, injury, or violence that makes them wary of their surroundings all the time. Suffice to say, it becomes difficult for them to control their emotions when they experience something similar.

- **Risky Behavior:** Teenagers and preteens are also becoming more and more careless about the activities they engage themselves in. From cyberbullying, engaging in unprotected sex, to becoming addicted to pornographic content, children are putting themselves at risk. Most of the time, risky behaviors become a venting outlet for children already suffering from some form of mental disorder.

- **Schizophrenia:** This is yet another type of mental health disorder where a child loses touch with reality. A schizophrenic individual experiences hallucinations, lack of motivation, disorganized speech, disordered thinking, delusion, and indulging in disruptive behaviors. A combination of genetic, physical, environmental, and psychological factors can make one more prone to developing it. Everyday stressors or chronic depression can also promote its onset.

- **Self-harm and Suicide:** Children who self-harm are at an increased risk of committing suicide in the future than those who don't. Although this doesn't necessarily guarantee their safety, research revealed that children that engaged in self-harming practicing were 30 times likelier to commit suicide in the future (Rodway et al., 2016). Thoughts about harming oneself result from depression and lack of affection. Children who feel like they aren't loved enough or repeatedly have troubling thoughts find suicide as an escape route from the cruelty of the world. They want to end the pain and suffering they experience all the time, and self-harm and suicide seems to be the only way.

There are some other often ignored but prevalent mental health conditions among youngsters. These include the following:

- **Narcissistic Personality Disorder:** When a child becomes a narcissist, they have an inflated sense of self-importance. They look down on others without any empathy in their eyes. Children with a narcissistic personality disorder are in constant need of attention and admiration that often puts them in troubled relationships with their friends, partners, and family.

- **Histrionic Personality Disorder:** In this type of mental health disorder, a child develops the habit of overdramatizing their feelings, emotions, and situation. They exaggerate the details deliberately to make their situation or feeling interesting. However, this is blatant lying and not a habit that should be encouraged.

- **Gaming Disorder:** Gaming disorder was only recently classified as a mental disorder by The World Health Organization. As it is similar to other forms of addictions, parents must be aware of the time their child spends playing video games. In this type of disorder, a child becomes obsessed with gaming. They give up on their sleep, eat junk food, don't get up for long hours, and hurt their eyes, shoulders, and neck in the process. Also, the exposure to guns, gambling, and causing havoc (damaging property, blowing up buildings, harassing strangers, etc.) becomes worrying.

Chapter 3:

Build Resilience

We often use the words resilience and mental toughness interchangeably. We assume they mean the same thing, but there is actually a slight difference between the two that we must understand so as to raise mentally strong children, not just resilient ones.

Resilience is a person's ability to bounce back quickly from a difficult event—both small and large. It doesn't necessarily point toward the individual developing a positive attitude. It is situational. One shows resilience when something goes awry. Then, if you have the strength to push past it, pick yourself up, and believe that you can overcome the loss and setback, that's called being resilient.

Mental strength, on the other hand, is a mindset that remains the same in both positive and negative situations. It's the strength within you. It isn't linked with some hardship that you face. It is the strength and willingness to be at your best at all times, even when life is going well.

In simpler terms, resilience is a defensive strategy. You can only build it when you have been knocked down.

Mental toughness is an offensive strategy, preventing you from getting knocked down in the first place.

But to build that kind of strength, resilience and confidence in your abilities is a must. This is why when we say that we want to raise mentally strong children, we need to work on building resilience as well as the confidence to fare well during difficult times.

As stated earlier, resilience is the ability to push past the setback and move forward. It involves struggle and hard work. Not everyone is cut to put in that amount of work. However, unlike other traits, resilience is a skill that means that it can be learned and taught. We can train our young ones to show resilience when they are pushed down instead of giving up.

Teenage years are difficult times for most children. The bodies are changing, crushes turn into lovers, and pressure from society increases. It's like suddenly we start to expect our children to know the best and be the best. However, we fail to understand that it's often the hardest to stay afloat when the waters are rocky— meaning that it's the time when they need us the most because so much is changing around them. All of a sudden, they are expected to find a job, get a place of their own, and pay their own bills. There is little navigation provided. Instead of telling them that it's okay to struggle and find a place where they fit in, we expect them to win and pick a career.

Since resilience is associated with bad times, we can't expect them to figure out everything on their own.

Sure, making mistakes is a great way to teach children, but it shouldn't be the *only* way. As parents, we should help them navigate through the difficult times they have and show them how to steer away from them without losing heart. We need to teach them how to overcome a failure and bounce back with increased motivation and dedication.

When children invest in the skills that go into being resilient, they can notice positive changes in their lives. They can learn to face any adversity on their own. This will alleviate the stress and anxiety that fills their brain. Less stress means a decreased chance of developing a mental health disorder as well as becoming mentally tough.

Why Is Resilience an Important Life Skill to Nurture?

Some children are naturally resilient. No matter what they have to face—difficult family situations, losing a loved one, learning disabilities, or physical handicaps— they just know how to get on with their lives. Then, some children are ready to put their hands in the air at the most trivial of misfortunes.

They view every small obstacle as an insurmountable stumbling block.

As parents, some of the blame is on us. We overdirect and overprotect. Without knowledge, we turn them into risk-averse rule followers. We discourage initiation and taking part in challenges. This puts a halt to their adaptability, flexibility, and curiosity. They fail to develop the survival skills they need to succeed tomorrow.

We reward them for memorizing all the right answers, but good grades aren't the only thing that would help them. It is their knowledge about the many life and social skills that will come in handy when they get down to the job. It comes down to how they make use of the content they are dished; evaluate; and then stitch it together with other information in ways that matter.

We also encourage competition which, in some cases, is healthy. However, competing for trophies and awards makes them want to win over everyone else. In the era that we are stepping in, collaboration is considered a big trait to have. In short, all that we were taught earlier holds little value. We need to raise them to be strong, confident, and self-sufficient. We need to raise people who will know what to do when they are faced with a difficult task.

Let's face it: Success in life isn't as simple as getting from point A to point B. Even when we make the most calculated steps, we stumble upon an unexpected setback. What we need to teach, therefore, is how to face that uncertainty and keep going. This is what makes them resilient—an important tool to becoming mentally strong.

What resilience will teach them are the following skills:

Competence

Competence doesn't mean mastery at school alone. It doesn't mean being good at every subject or sport. Competence is about building skills, too. It is about learning about new things, taking on new challenges, and being your best. Resilience allows children to gather the courage to take part in new and different things because they aren't afraid of failing. Neither are they afraid that they will be made fun of.

Confidence

Children who are confident in their abilities can have increased feelings of hope, resilience, optimism, and efficacy. Resilience combined with confidence makes children do well in exams and be happier about the opportunities ahead of them. They also have the grit to bounce back and overcome failure.

Connection

Resilience teaches children and youngsters about social connections and how to form them. Resilient children have a strong bond with the people closest to them— these include family members, siblings, friends, and educators. They feel loved and validated which is what gives them the strength to overcome anything in life. It is because they know that they can count on their supportive network when in need.

Contribution

Resilience also teaches young ones about how their actions make a positive difference in society and the world. If they have an idea, they simply keep the idea for themselves. They want to improve the lives of others. They want to come up with solutions that would facilitate the lives of those in need. Resilience makes them goal-oriented individuals. It empowers them to stay committed to making a difference with their hard work. This realization is what makes them keep going and achieving their end goals.

Control

Resilient children have more control over their lives and decisions. When you teach a little one about resilience, you teach them about responsibility and owning up to their mistakes. You teach them accountability of their actions and how it affects the lives of others. The more in control they are of their actions and decisions, the more confident they feel in all their endeavors. Also, control promotes predictability. Children who have stable routines, clear expectations, and clear boundaries are less likely to be stressed because there is little unpredictability.

Overcome Fears Together

To raise resilient children, the first thing you need to do is teach them how to overcome their fears. If they are the kind that gives up easily, it is because they are scared of being shamed or ridiculed. They fear being labeled a failure. They are scared that this label will become the very definition of who they are.

Ask yourself this: How will they learn if they never fail? How will they know the value of success if they never taste failure? How will they celebrate something they achieved if they never knew what losing felt like? To become resilient, they need to overcome the fears that prevent them from taking action—any of it. They need to put their negative thoughts to rest and step out of their comfort zones.

Below are some ideas to help you teach them how their fears aren't bigger than their goals.

Grit Interviews

Children look up to their parents, grandparents, and older siblings. They want to be like them. They think they have it all, but that "all" didn't come to them easily. They had to work hard for it. Let your child know of the struggles and setbacks their role models had to face before becoming successful in their lives. Prepare interview questions with them to ask their role models who have achieved something in their lives through their honest work.

Knowing about their stories, experiences, and struggles will teach them more about grit and resilience than any good book you can find in a store. Emphasize the benefits of following their passions and having perseverance.

You can also read biographies to them of famous people who stumbled upon many roadblocks before becoming successful. Examples like J.K. Rowling having her book rejected a dozen times before a publication house decided to print it or about how Oprah was told that she was too ugly to be on TV will surely inspire young minds to stay persistent in difficult times and overcome any setback they encounter.

Controlled Exposure

Gradually helping young children come face-to-face with their fears is another smart strategy. Some situations that provoke anxiety act as triggers to release stress hormones in the body. This can be prevented if the individual's fear is gradually overcome. Controlled exposure can eventually foster resilience. It can also help children have the courage to face their worst fears. Once they overcome some fears with your help, they will gradually learn how to take care of them on their own. For example, if your child is afraid of going into the water, controlled exposure will allow them to progressively defeat their fear. You can sign up for some basic classes at first in knee-deep waters and then steadily increase the level of the water as they become more confident in their swimming.

"What Makes Me Strong?"

This is a fun game for not just the child but everyone in the house. Often, the reason children have fears is that they underestimate their abilities and talents to overcome them. They don't think they have it in them to ever step out in the light and conquer their fears. This activity helps you and others remind them of their strengths. Learning about their strengths will shift their pessimistic thinking into constructive and happy thoughts. They will feel important, valued, and confident. This activity will help them recognize what traits make them the strongest. Make sure to label these traits as gifts that they have.

Start with asking everyone to gather around and hand them a sheet of paper. The paper should contain a list of traits and talents like modesty, patience, creativity, consideration, kindness, compassion, empathy, etc. Ask everyone to circle the skills they think they possess. Point out that they will have to be honest and sure about who they are, as they would have to explain the reasons why they think that.

Once done, ask every member to take turns talking about their gifts and how those gifts fit them. Then, pass on the sheets and ask all members to make additions to the sheet of paper they have in hand. For example, if you have your spouse's sheet and you think that they should have circled more traits than they did,

circle them and communicate it to everyone.
Sometimes, it is easier to believe others than ourselves.

Chapter 4:

Talk About Feelings

Being a parent comes with its own set of challenges. Every child is different and has different traits, habits, and nature. Some are naturally tough and others aren't. Some like to throw tantrums and have meltdowns while others keep things bottled up inside. Although both these strategies don't do well in the long run, there is a technique that can help both equally: self-regulation. Self-regulation is the art of learning to manage your emotions yourself. It is a skill that can be taught and should be a "must" in the parent training program. The struggle around inappropriate behavior, use of foul language, and expressing oneself in awkward and harmful ways is real, and surely parents can fare well with some training about self-regulation in the early developmental stages.

As stated before, self-regulation talks about how well one regulates their emotions and behaviors according to any given situation. There are some instances where one forgets all about emotional regulation like a highly stressful or triggering situation, but as for the other times, preteens and teenagers should know how to cope with their negative thoughts and overwhelming thoughts before reacting to them. Self-regulation also looks at how one can resist highly emotional reactions, calm themselves down, not get upset, adjust to a change, and tackle frustration without having a meltdown. Since it is still so viable in today's time, it is sensible to go about nurturing it in young minds.

A well-rounded teen can gain a lot from self-regulation. They can learn to remain calm and build focus without losing their confidence. This will help them stay mentally strong and get out of any stressful situation gracefully.

Empower Kids to Take Charge of Their Emotions

Research reveals that major changes take place in the brain's architecture during adolescence, too. Earlier, it was believed that most of the learning and building of skills happened from the time a child was a toddler to when they were a preteen. However, there is still some room left for molding better habits and talents. During adolescence, the brain system seeks reward and processes feelings better than cognitive control systems—stimulating good decision making and future planning.

What this means is that self-regulation during this time is developmentally out of balance, but progress is there, and so is some work that can be strengthened with support and instruction. Teenagers who have had a history of adverse early childhood experiences can make use of this and gain more control of their emotions, feelings, and thoughts. They can also control their responses to stressful situations and become more confident in how they express themselves.

Mental strength doesn't mean that one won't have any emotions. It isn't about building a strong outward facade. It's about improved honing and how one stays calm and composed despite being triggered. Having mental strength means that one can acknowledge their emotions and manage them as they come. Therefore, to cultivate mental toughness, you need to raise children that are empowered and can self-regulate. You need to offer them the right tools and strategies to help them make sense of what they are feeling and what would be an appropriate reaction to it.

To do so, the first step involves helping them acknowledge what they are feeling. They don't need to shy away and hide their tears when they see an emotional scene in a movie. They don't need to act all tough and strong when they're breaking on the inside. They don't need to act as if nothing gets to them. Telling them to mask their feelings damages their ability to process their emotions well.

Tell them that it's okay to acknowledge what they are going through. If they feel unsure and remain socially bound to act a certain way, let them know that you don't approve of it. In your house, they have the right to be who they want to be. They shouldn't have to hide who they are. It's as simple as saying, "I understand that you're mad because I'm not allowing you to have that chocolate. I know you're frustrated because it smells so delicious."

Once you acknowledge their feelings, they have a label for it. The knowledge itself can act as a calming strategy. It tells the child that they are being understood. What follows next are some practical techniques to help them get over their emotions in the healthiest ways possible.

Cool-Down Area

Set up a cool-down area in your house if you have young children. They love the idea of having some space to themselves, let alone a corner where they can unwind and release bad energy. A cool-down area offers refuge from negative emotions like frustration, anger, sadness, or anxiety. Going into that space alone starts the act of processing thoughts. You can decorate it together with your child and help them understand its use. In the beginning, whenever you catch them being sad, angry, or irritated, instill the idea that they can go to the cool-down area and feel calm again. There, you can also set up their favorite activities or set up a shelf full of their favorite books and CDs. The walls can also be decorated with positive affirmations. The available stationery can include color therapy books, colors, markers, and stress balls.

If they are older, it will be easier to make them understand how they can utilize the corner and find a release for their emotions. They can pick scented candles known to calm one's mind and improve mood. If they play an instrument, you can set up a little studio for them, too. The idea is to help them find a place where they can learn to be with their emotions themselves and decide how they want to deal with them.

Discuss Scenarios

Talking about different types of emotions and how they can affect one's mental well-being can also be accomplished by role-playing different scenarios. For example, if you notice them being sad, you can initiate by sharing a made-up story about how someone you respected and loved let you down and how that made you feel. If they look angry, you can come up with a story where someone deceived you or took advantage of your niceness.

Similarly, you can then ask them for advice as to what you should do next or what they would have done if they were in a similar spot. They will have some brilliant ideas on how to move past the anger and deceit. While you're at it, make sure to stress the fact that venting it out with you made you feel a lot calmer. This will signal them to do the same whenever they feel like they need to have a heart-to-heart with someone.

Chapter 5:

Encourage Positive Self-

Expression

Self-expression is the art of expressing yourself in a way you feel comfortable with. It can include your words, facial expressions, movement, body, action, clothes, and possessions. Self-expression reveals a lot about your inner authentic self.

The idea, at its very core, sounds simple, but it is only because rarely any of us grasp the importance of it. From early childhood, we have been fed messages about the way we should dress, sit, eat, or walk. Men have been told to toughen up, and women have been scolded for not sitting like a lady. Then, when school started, we were told off to stay away from a certain group of people and hang out with the "normal" kids instead. Later, we were told to pick subjects we never liked and make careers out of them. When it came down to finding someone to love, there were a whole lot of terms and conditions on that, too.

The constant missives about what to do and what not to do shaped our personality. If given a chance today, many of us would have chosen different career paths. We would have stuck to something that we enjoyed doing instead.

Luckily, we are now in the position to do just that for our children, and mind you, this is an important task. Allowing children the power of self-expression is the best gift you can give to them. Self-expression is what would lead them to find fulfillment in their lives. It is what would make them the happiest, most radiant souls in the world. It will help them reach their true potential without being ever told to be someone else. Only then can they make a difference in the world!

All they need to do is reframe their negative thoughts with positive ones. Use the power of "yet" and know that they can master anything they want to. This is also true about how they want to express themselves. Sometimes, children have a hard time being true to themselves. They feel pressured into acting as the perfect specimen all the time. They have to pretend to be someone else because they fear no one would like the real them. With all this going on in their head, how can you expect them to become mentally strong? How can you expect them to be true to themselves when they fear stigmatization?

Promoting Positive Self-Talk

Being expressive and thinking positively can help them get through difficult times and be themselves. It can help them perform at their best. Below are three strategies to encourage that sort of positive self-expression and thinking.

Positive Affirmations

Positive self-talk or affirmations are a great way to deal with the stresses of life without losing your cool. Positive affirmations don't work like magic but do have a compelling effect on how one views themselves. Practicing daily affirmations yourself and encouraging your child to try and do the same can help them overcome their fears, build confidence, gain resilience, and become mentally tough.

Simply ask them to craft their list of positive affirmations and put it up in a place where they can repeat them daily. Let them know that regardless of what others think about them, it is their thinking and perception that matters the most. If they feel confident in who they are, no one can bring them down.

Art Therapy

Any form of art—be it dance, playing an instrument, painting, writing, or dressing the way they want to—is considered art therapy. Since movement has been linked with the release of dopamine, the happiness-inducing chemicals in the brain, dancing or exercising can become a great way to express yourself and find the release of emotions that have been bottled up inside. Dancing your heart out to your favorite beats can become a way to channel positive thoughts.

Children can take advantage of it too and express themselves in their unique way. They can also keep a feelings journal where they write about their feelings. They can also be expressive with how they dress. If they are creative, colorful, and optimistic, they can choose more vibrant colors in their attire and feel good about themselves. They can paint or sketch images they resonate with.

All About Me

This final activity involves creating a worksheet that is simple and fun to complete. Again, the idea is to promote self-expression and also help them reframe their negative thoughts. You start by asking them for their name, date of birth, best friend's name, place of birth, etc. in the first section.

In the next section, you move on to discovering their likes/dislikes, preferences, and interests such as what is their favorite thing for breakfast, favorite movie, favorite places to visit, a favorite pastime, etc.

In the final section, encourage creative and thoughtful answers where they have to spend a few minutes contemplating their answers. For example, you can ask them to remember a time when they had the most fun, what things/people bring a smile to their face instantly, the one thing they would change in the world if they were made president for a day, etc.

You can turn this into a weekly or monthly activity where you come up with innovative questions every time to promote positive self-expression.

Chapter 6:

Let Them Make Mistakes

When children get the opportunity to struggle and fail, they develop many important life and emotional skills. They realize that, at the end of the day, it is themselves that have to brush off the dust and get up. The emotions that accompany that mistake or struggle are their own, and how they deal with them is also a product of their mind.

As parents, we often rush to save them from all harm. We see them pouring cereal in their bowl and hurriedly do it for them so that they won't pour it all over the place. We see them pulling the hair of another child despite being told not to, and we run to separate them before the other child decides to respond. We see them struggling to provide a caretaker with their name out of shyness, and we answer for them. This sounds protective and maybe too much like a parent, but what if we let them struggle for some time and let them bear the consequences that follow? There is a lot that they can learn from the mistakes they make and the consequences that come with them.

As parents, our role should be more of a support and guide. We shouldn't do things out of love because they won't learn to do them on their own. We have to instill in them the belief that they can do whatever they want to. If they don't develop the skills that they need to survive right now, they will have a difficult time learning them when they become adults.

They will fail, cry, show anger, and be frustrated . . . but they will also learn. They will learn that not everything turns out perfect all the time. They will learn that they will have setbacks in life and will have to deal with them on their own. Making mistakes will teach them how to become independent and self-reliant. Isn't that the ultimate goal of every parenting practice?

It's to raise them with the belief that they have the ultimate power to do whatever they want in their lives, despite the failures they incur.

Learning is enriched through error. It doesn't matter if it involves navigating new friendships, setting healthy boundaries, homework, getting better at the catch, or developing a healthy habit—learning happens when children think creatively. When they learn to solve problems, they learn to take the lead. Learning from mistakes is, therefore, an important part because it challenges young minds to do things differently. It encourages them to try new ways and innovative approaches to resolving their issues. Learning from mistakes helps develop good judgment and increases wisdom.

By allowing them to make mistakes, you teach them how to deal with the daily stresses in life and develop customized coping mechanisms for them. For example, some might feel like punching a punching bag releases stress. Others might listen to their favorite band or spend some time alone in silence. This builds resilience and mental toughness. This also prepares them to overcome negative experiences.

In short, the more mistakes a child makes, the more they learn. The mistakes work as stepping-stones toward a happier and healthier life that they can build for themselves when they continue to learn and improve. According to psychologist Deborah Zlotnik, children who fear making mistakes are more worried, at a greater risk of having anxiety disorders, and are less likely to try new experiences (Jones, 2019).

Does Our Reaction Matter?

One of the biggest reasons children fear making mistakes is because they are afraid of your reaction. So what if they spilled some milk on the floor or folded the clean laundry wrong? These things can happen to even the most careful of us. When children fear that they will be scolded if they did something wrong, they stop trying altogether. They become lazy in taking initiative.

Knowing how to respond to your child's mistakes or failures is an important skill that you need to nurture in yourself. From being patient to understanding, they need you to be on their side when things go awry. Regardless of the fact that they lost a match, got bad grades, or had trouble following basic instructions, how you react in those situations is important for your child's healthy mental and emotional development.

Your poor reactions can have a lasting impact on how they process failures. When they see you disappointed in them, they start to doubt their intelligence. They start believing that they aren't good enough and give up on themselves.

Children will have learning adventures no matter how cautious they are—they are children, after all. What you can do instead of showing anger or disappointment in them is to help them embrace it. This will teach them to remain accountable for what they did and do better the next time. It won't take away their confidence or their eagerness to try. Shaming them would do so.

For starters, know whether you are setting a good example or not. How are you handling your mistakes? Do you own up to them or do you pretend they never happened? Do you yell, swear, or sulk? Do you blame others for making a mess? What a child sees you do is what they will pick up. Therefore, teach by example. Be as perfect of a role model as you can be—the one that isn't afraid of making mistakes and doesn't see any harm in making them.

Second, learn to pick your battles. Some mistakes can be laughed off. This means that you have to maintain your calm and get over them. Holding your child accountable for putting the wrong shoes on and then berating them throughout the ride won't do anyone good. Your job is to ensure that they learn to make good choices, and it can only happen when you let them work through their bad choice and laugh it off.

Show affection when they seem disheartened. Sometimes, children lose heart because they know that they could have done a better job. When you see that they appear truly remorseful and guilty, let the angry parent take a seat. Showing affection suggests that you love them regardless, and it acts as the perfect dose of encouragement that they need.

Don't set expectations too high. If your child gets average grades in school, don't expect them to become the top student in their class next year. Progress takes time and happens gradually. With every mistake that your child makes, they learn something new. Let go of the idea of perfection, and let kids be kids. Being too rigid with your reactions will make them afraid of making a blunder. It can also affect the loving relationship between you two because the child will start to keep secrets from you because of your responses. We aren't perfect either, so what makes us the judge in putting that type of pressure on our little ones?

Finally, praise effort. No matter how small, progress is progress. If you know that your child did their best and still incurred failure, don't forget to praise them for the effort. Right now, they need to hear it from you more than ever. Let them know that you're proud of them for trying and prouder for accepting their mistakes.

How to Teach Children to Embrace Mistakes and Move Forward

Depending on the type of mistake and circumstance, you can decide how you want to address it and help your child take accountability for it. You may choose to offer better solutions if they seem disheartened or simply comfort them. You may speak about what happened and go over the details of where things went wrong. Whichever strategy you choose, make sure that you know that your child is doing well.

As for the teaching part, below are some ideas to foster acceptance and accountability for the mistakes and help them move on.

Project: Made by Mistake

Since learning from mistakes isn't automatic and every child feels ashamed of making mistakes in the first place, this serves as an amazing activity (aka, a research project) for preteens and teenagers. For this particular project, ask your child to come up with a list of things that were invented by mistake. A list of accidental things may look something like this:

- **Penicillin:** A scientist called Sir Alexander Fleming accidentally left a contaminated Petri dish uncovered before leaving his lab. The next day, he came to find some mold in it that was eating up all the bacteria around it. He grew the mold and later discovered that it contained an antibiotic: penicillin (Gaynes, 2017).

- **Slinky:** A naval engineer Richard Jones was working with tension springs when one of them fell on the ground. Since it kept bouncing on its own, it became a fun yet accidental discovery ("Slinky," 2021).

- **Potato Chips:** A customer kept returning their potato fries to the kitchen, wanting to have them crispier and fried a bit extra. Out of sheer anger, the chef, George Crum, sliced them very thin and fried them until they turned golden brown. All we know is that the customer loved it and so do we!

See? Collecting this type of information is both fun and reassuring. It also teaches children that not all mistakes are failures. There is a lot that one can learn from them.

See the Silver Lining Together

A lot of times, children quit because their efforts didn't yield the results they wanted. They view their failure as a failure alone, but we know that a failure can be a great teacher, too. This is what we have to make them see. Schedule sessions where you two talk about the things that went wrong, and make them point out the silver lining in it. For example, if they didn't make it to the sports team despite giving their best, let it be known that at least they got to practice and learned so many new tricks in the process. That, in itself, is an amazing accomplishment. Encourage that they keep practicing and honing those tricks to become the best player there is and increase their chances of getting selected the next time.

Similarly, if they got dumped by a partner, show them how the whole experience of dating was a great lesson to become a better partner. If they know of the reasons for which they were dumped, don't feel hesitant in bringing them up and discussing them. Knowing about those reasons is the first step toward improvement. Had their partner settled with them regardless of their negative ways, your child would have never learned about them. If they never learned about them, they would have never had the chance to improve.

"What Do You Think?"

This isn't an activity but more of an exercise that you do with your child whenever they come to you with a question or task. Ask them to try first. If they fail, let them have another try at it and then another. In the meantime, run them through the process of how it's done without doing it for them. For example, if they are young and want you to tie their shoelaces, say, "Let me first see you try it. I know you can." Then, when they fail, add a small instruction to facilitate them without physically helping. The goal is to help them see that learning happens after they have made a mistake and not before. It also tells them that trying is the only way to perfect something.

Chapter 7:

Encourage Problem-Solving and Taking Responsibility

Problem-solving is a learned skill that involves finding creative and innovative means to do something. This comes in handy, especially when one feels like they are about to give up. The motivation to keep going and come up with new solutions for the same problems is what makes this a wholesome skill to nurture in children.

All children are naturally inquisitive. They have many questions to ask you daily about anything that interests them. From seeking permission to do something to tell you that they have done something already, their inquisitive nature and curiosity make their world exciting. These questions improve their comprehension and understanding of various things and why they are a certain way. Yet this curiosity is unintentionally executed in children by their parents, friends, and educators. Since "no" is the most common word they hear, they develop a fear of trying new things. They fear that they will hurt themselves. They fear shame, guilt, and humiliation. They fear that they will disappoint others. They fear that their parents won't like it, so they gradually stop asking questions, and after some time, they stop altogether.

However, this also stops the process of discovery and exploration. When they don't have anything interesting to think about or do, there are no new problems to solve. This also means that the brain has nothing to feel challenged and active about.

Thus, problem-solving is an important life skill to instill in children so that they can become leaders of tomorrow. With their inquisitiveness and curiosity, they can make a positive contribution to the world and their community. They can become trailblazers, cure chronic diseases, and win medals for their country. It all begins when they start to think differently about something and focus on the improvisation of processes.

Stop Spoon-Feeding Solutions

Spoon-feeding is something that a parent does and later regrets doing when their child is unable to survive without them or their partner's presence when they grow up. The concept emerges from the idea when children are babies and rely on their parents, especially the mother, for every basic thing. From changing diapers to feeding, the mother does everything for the child until they learn to take care of themselves. However, some mothers never stop spoon-feeding even when the child becomes mature enough to take responsibility, and that is where things start to go wrong.

There are several reasons why spoon-feeding isn't a recommended practice. Parents who spoon-feed their children take away their power to think or do things themselves. It's like parents taking off the burden from their back to make their lives easier without realizing the damage they are doing. Children that lack basic life skills like communication, social interaction, personal hygiene, or having the power to decide something for themselves, get accustomed to this type of parental "help" all the time. When they grow older, have to move out, and make a place for themselves in the world, they have immense trouble doing that. It's because they have never done it before and don't have the skills needed for it. An example of this can look like a teenager that asks their parents for money, doesn't know how to cook, or cleans after themselves.

Other disadvantages of spoon-feeding involve raising a lazy thinker. A child that doesn't take interest in initiation, creativity, or problem-solving remains behind other children that do. Spoon-fed children only take an interest in doing what they have been asked or told to do without going the extra mile. They stick to what they know and never feel the zest to step into the unknown and discover something new. They focus solely on the learning that has been prescribed to them. For example, a child might only learn about what's in the textbook without looking at any reference books for better comprehension. They also don't understand the reasons why they are doing something. These children develop a herd instinct which means that they are incompetent to think outside the box or have an opinion of their own.

If they are never encouraged to gather more information about something, the current information in their mind will become of no use either. As they won't have any opinion themselves, they will have a hard time researching and forming an opinion about something. Think of it as being told to write about a subject you do not know of, like politics. Whatever information you will gather will come from different sources and other people. You won't have a thought of your own because you never made the effort to research about it yourself.

Spoon-feeding, as stated earlier, prevents the development of essential problem-solving skills. If a child is never encouraged to take charge and think imaginatively, they won't know what to do when they come across an unexpected situation. They will never be in a position to lead and will always wait for instructions from others before doing something.

There is also a risk to their mental health because they only consume information coming from passive sources and not their mind. Even when they think that what they are doing is wrong, they will do it because they don't know what else to do. Also, in the lack of your presence or instruction, such a child would feel helpless and depressed. Anxiety will take over and wreck things and relationships for them. Failure caused by this will lead to poor self-esteem and self-worth.

When children become habituated to be on the receiving end of things only, they can never conclude a creative result. They will always do things by the book and never have the curiosity to try something new and different. For example, a child that is spoon-fed won't have the desire to answer a question on the exam creatively. They will only resort to the crammed version of the answer and not be innovative with examples straight from their mind. They will also accept the final assessment without argument because there is no true motivation in learning.

That being said, if you are a smart parent that wants to raise mentally strong and confident children, give your child the chance to practice their talents and skills. These skills should allow them to experience discomfort and encourage thinking outside the box. This doesn't suggest that you purposely expose them to circumstances out of their control to toughen them up but rather stop taking over their life. Let them be bored, disappointed, and frustrated. Let them experience the stress that comes from being told to lead. Let them feel scared of not knowing what to do. Only then will they become brave and confident. Only then will they learn the true value of winning and success.

Let Them Take Charge

Let them be the captain of their ship. Let them sail through the huge waves without counsel or guidance. Offer support and encouragement, but let them try on their own. Sooner or later, they are going to take control of their lives, and the sooner they learn how to be independent and look after their needs, the better. Below are some ideas to help them be brave about leading and problem-solving.

What Is the Worst That Could Happen?

Minimizing the worst-case scenario can help children feel more confident about taking charge. Be it delivering a speech in class, performing in a play, asking someone for prom, etc., are all examples of situations that your child might find themselves in. Their anxiety might take over and make them lose all their confidence. However, this can be prevented if the child is aware of the worst- and best-case scenarios. Worst-case scenario thinking is common among children. A slight inconvenience is enough to convince them that their world is over. Here's how you can prevent this sort of catastrophizing from happening.

Ask your child to bring a piece of paper and a pen. Divide the paper into two columns. Title the first column as the "Worst-Case Scenario" and the second as the "Best-Case Scenario." Next, ask your child to list down all their concerns and worries about what might happen if they take charge of something in the first column. Next, ask them to envision the best things that would come out of it and how it would make them feel. Doing so will make them come to terms with what they have to gain and lose if they choose to take charge of something. A simple list of the worst- and best-case scenarios will diffuse most of the intensity of the thinking. They will realize that their concerns aren't as big and worrisome as they thought them to be. Most of them will be highly unlikely to happen.

Be Clear

Being clear and concise with your instructions when you want them to take charge is another valuable strategy that works wonders. When a child knows what is expected of them, it acts as a guideline for them. They take charge with more confidence because they know what they are expected to encounter. Being concise is also important because if there are too many steps, it can create confusion and prevent action out of fear. For example, if you want them to take part in helping you with the chores, be clear about what you expect them to do. If you want them to set the table for dinner, show them where the dishes are, how they should place the mats, and what dishes they should use for serving the meals.

Breathe

Initiation is always a difficult concept for beginners. Some are never that confident to take charge. However, there is an easy way to help calm the nerves and stay in control: breathing. A simple act that we do every second of the day is a great exercise to start with. However, the breathing we are talking about here is breathing to manage anxiety. This, of course, takes practice and requires one to stay present and vigilant. Deep breathing has been a go-to strategy for Buddhists and monks who are experts at taking control of every thought that crosses their minds. Since taking charge comes with its challenges and negative emotions, it is natural for a child to feel stress.

Five minutes of breathing exercises for children where they hold their breath for a few seconds and then release it slowly is a perfect start to their day. If they are too young, ask them to count until three before exhaling. They can increase the number of seconds as they pick up speed. Encourage children to practice it every time they fear something. Doing so primes the system to respond more efficiently. It prevents the body from producing cortisol—the stress hormone.

Conclusion

Mentally strong children are confident and creative. They have a mind of their own that doesn't believe in failure. They anticipate setbacks and failures and see them as a part of their growth and development. They try, try, and try without giving up. They understand that the only way to learn something new is by practicing and perfecting it.

Raising mentally strong children in a world that continues to shock us with its opinionated and unjust views about mental health issues prevalent among youngsters is difficult. The reason for that is that we are one of the first ones to offer criticism. It isn't always intentional but something that has been molded into us. We stereotype things because we have been raised that way. We have trouble seeing things differently and accepting new perspectives. But we don't have to make our children become the same. We can put an end to this stereotyping and raise them to be independent, mentally tough, and confident adults. We can teach them how to carry themselves well, manage their emotions, and learn to accept and own up to their mistakes.

As parents, it should be our goal to educate ourselves and others about the many prevailing mental health problems that our children face daily without disregarding them. Education happens when we understand the many signs and symptoms and learn about various disorders that could be the reason why your preteen or teenager acts a certain way. Only when we comprehend these and notice the signs can we be in the position to help.

What follows next is building resilience. Having the ability to bounce back from adversities and face the world confidently is another important life skill that we must cultivate. They should take on new challenges with confidence and deal with any setbacks, and this can only happen when they have the grit to move on.

Next, we must teach them about emotional regulation so that they can manage their reactions to the everyday stresses in their lives. From heartbreaks to not getting a job they wanted so badly, they are going to be disappointed and experience frustrations when things don't go as planned. In such circumstances, it is very easy to lose sight of future goals and give in to negative emotions and feelings. Young ones must be taught to be sensible and act maturely. They should be given instructions about healthy coping strategies so that they can control how emotions affect them.

Then, they must also be taught to make mistakes and embrace them so that the process of learning doesn't stop. They should also know how to own up to their mistakes and make amends. This is possible when parents stop taking over.

Finally, we must know that we can only raise a problem-solver if we forgo the idea of offering help and spoon-feeding them answers. They should get acquainted with the discomforts in life and know that they can happen to the best of us.

Hopefully, having followed these steps, you can raise children to become mentally strong and self-reliant adults who are confident of who they are and their abilities and talents. They know how to embrace their mistakes and losses and continue to make progress despite that.

Thank you for giving this book a read. I hope you loved reading it as much as I enjoyed writing it. It would make me the happiest person on earth if you would take a moment to leave an honest review. All you have to do is visit the site where you purchased this book: It's that simple! The review doesn't have to be a full-fledged paragraph; a few words will do. Your few words will help others decide if this is what they should be reading as well. Thank you in advance, and best of luck with your parenting adventures. Every moment is a joyous one with a child.

References

15+ strategies to help build self-regulation skills - the pathway 2 success. (2018, November 5). Pathway 2 Success. https://www.thepathway2success.com/15-strategies-to-help-build-self-regulation-skills/

Ackerman, C. E. (2018, August 6). *What is self-expression and how to foster it? (20 activities + examples)*. PositivePsychology.com. https://positivepsychology.com/self-expression/

Ackerman, C. E. (2019, June 21). *27 resilience activities and worksheets for students and adults (+pdfs)*. PositivePsychology.com. https://positivepsychology.com/resilience-activities-worksheets/

Addressing Stigma. (n.d.). The Center for Addiction and Mental Health [CAMH].

https://www.camh.ca/en/driving-change/addressing-stigma

Adolescent mental health. (2020, September 28). Who.int; World Health Organization: WHO. https://www.who.int/news-room/fact-sheets/detail/adolescent-mental-health

Brukner, L. (2021, May 24). *Emotional regulation activities for tweens and teens.* Edutopia. https://www.edutopia.org/article/emotional-regulation-activities-tweens-and-teens

Christina. (2018, August 9). *Turning mistakes into opportunities for learning.* Mrs. Winter's Bliss. https://mrswintersbliss.com/turning-mistakes-into-opportunities-for-learning/

Cullins, A. (n.d.). *9 activities to build grit and resilience in children.* Big Life Journal. https://biglifejournal.com/blogs/blog/activities-grit-resilience-children

Davies, P. (2021, February 1). *3 reasons "spoon feeding" your child doesn't help their development.* Moms.

https://www.moms.com/spoon-feeding-harmful-child-development/

Daugherty, G. (2021, February 3). *Who Invented the Potato Chip?* History. https://www.history.com/news/who-invented-potato-chip-saratoga

Etcheson, S. (2021, August 2). *The importance of educating family members about mental health.* Step up for Mental Health. https://www.stepupformentalhealth.org/the-importance-of-educating-family-members-about-mental-health/

Gaynes, R. (2017). The Discovery of Penicillin—New Insights After More Than 75 Years of Clinical Use. *Emerging Infectious Diseases, 23*(5), 849–853. https://doi.org/10.3201/eid2305.161556

Green, C. R. (2019, July 24). *Understanding resilience and mental toughness.* Medium. https://connieragengreen.medium.com/understanding-resilience-and-mental-toughness-9c0cf643b0d9

Huntley, A. (2011, December 8). *When children make mistakes*. The Idea Room. https://www.theidearoom.net/when-children-make-mistakes/

Jones, A. (2019, December 17). *It's hard, but your kids *seriously* benefit when you let them make mistakes*. Romper. https://www.romper.com/p/let-your-child-make-mistakes-for-these-7-benefits-experts-say-19454963

Lee, K. (2021, January 31). *How should you react when your child makes a mistake?* Verywell Family. https://www.verywellfamily.com/what-to-do-when-your-child-makes-a-mistake-4050012

Levine, M. (2020). *Ready or not : Preparing our kids to thrive in an uncertain and rapidly changing world*. Harper, An Imprint Of Harpercollins Publishers.

McCarthy, C. (2019, November 20). *Anxiety in Teens is Rising: What's Going On?* Healthychildren.org. https://www.healthychildren.org/English/health-issues/conditions/emotional-problems/Pages/Anxiety-Disorders.aspx

Mead, S. (2019). *7 key characteristics of resilient children.*
Whitbyschool.org.
https://www.whitbyschool.org/passionforlearn
ing/7-key-characteristics-of-resilient-children

Monroe, J. (2018, October 30). *A guide to teen mental
disorders.* Newport Academy; Newport
Academy.
https://www.newportacademy.com/resources/
mental-health/teen-mental-disorders/

Morin, A. (2020, October 3). *The critical difference between
mental strength and resilience, according to a
psychotherapist.* Business Insider.
https://www.businessinsider.com/the-critical-
difference-between-mental-strength-and-
resilience-2020-9

Murray, D. W., & Rosanbalm, K. (2017). *Promoting self-
regulation in adolescents and young adults: A practice
brief.*
https://fpg.unc.edu/sites/fpg.unc.edu/files/res
ources/reports-and-policy-
briefs/Promoting%20Self-

Regulation%20in%20Adolescents%20and%20Y
oung%20Adults.pdf

Pietro, S. (2016, October 31). *How can we help kids with self-regulation?* Child Mind Institute; Child Mind Institute. https://childmind.org/article/can-help-kids-self-regulation/

Ribeiro, M. (2019, July 4). *How to become mentally strong: 14 strategies for building resilience.* PositivePsychology.com. https://positivepsychology.com/mentally-strong/

Rodway, C., Tham, S.-G., Ibrahim, S., Turnbull, P., Windfuhr, K., Shaw, J., Kapur, N., & Appleby, L. (2016). Suicide in children and young people in england: A consecutive case series. *The Lancet Psychiatry, 3*(8), 751–759. https://doi.org/10.1016/s2215-0366(16)30094-3

Samoray, C. (2019, March 29). *UMD college of education | news.* Education.umd.edu. https://education.umd.edu/news/03-29-19-

parental-involvement-%E2%80%9Cprotective-factor%E2%80%9D-mental-health

Slinky. (2021, August 18). In *Wikipedia.*
https://en.wikipedia.org/wiki/Slinky#

Strycharczyk, D. (2015, July 31). *Resilience and mental toughness: Is there a difference and does it mat.* Kogan Page.
https://www.koganpage.com/article/resilience-and-mental-toughness-is-there-a-difference-and-does-it-matter

Worried about changes in your child's mood or behavior? (2018). Mayo Clinic.
https://www.mayoclinic.org/healthy-lifestyle/childrens-health/in-depth/mental-illness-in-children/art-20046577

Your child's mental health. (2017, May).
Www.caringforkids.cps.ca.
https://www.caringforkids.cps.ca/handouts/mentalhealth/mental_health

Zelas, C. (2021, August 18). *Parenting techniques for raising resilient children.* LI Press. https://www.longislandpress.com/2021/08/18/parenting-techniques-for-raising-resilient-children/

Made in the USA
Coppell, TX
03 September 2023

21156476R00044